ILLUSTRATED ENCYCLOPEDIA
SCIENCE

Managing Editor: Dr. Geeta Rani Arora
Editor: Ms. Pawanpreet Kaur
Education Consultant: Dr. Bimla Arora, *Shemrock School*

Pegasus
An imprint of
B. Jain Publishers (P) Ltd.
USA - EUROPE - INDIA

What is science?

Science is the knowledge of the physical and biological world. Science is also the systematic study of the physical world that can be verified through observations, measurements and experiments. The word 'science' is derived from the Latin word, *scientia* which means "knowledge."

Branches of Science

Science is divided into different fields of study. Physics, chemistry and biology are the major branches of science. Other branches include geography, geology, resource sciences, environmental science, astronomy, biotechnology, engineering, computer and information technology, microbiology, nutrition, and applied sciences.

Quick Look

Environmental science is the study of the interaction between the physical, chemical and biological components of the environment.

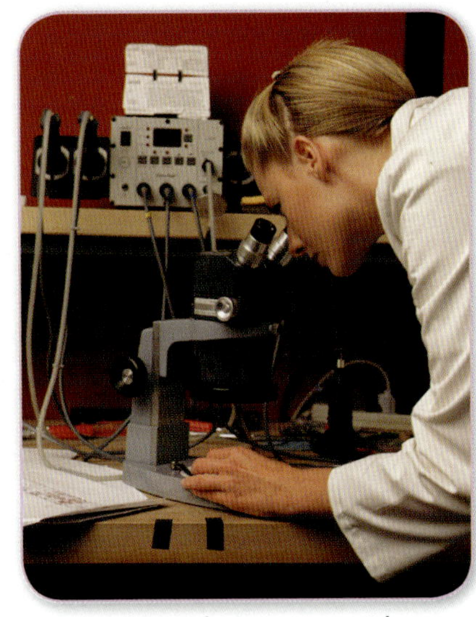

Laboratory is an exclusive room with necessary apparatuses and instruments where scientists conduct experiments.

Biotechnology is used in agriculture, brewing and baking.

Weather stations measure air pressure, wind speed, temperature, and precipitation.

Meteorology

Meteorology is the science of the atmosphere. Meteorology studies the atmosphere and atmospheric phenomena. It also studies the atmosphere's interaction with the earth's surface and oceans. Meteorologists collect information and forecast weather from weather stations located both on land and sea.

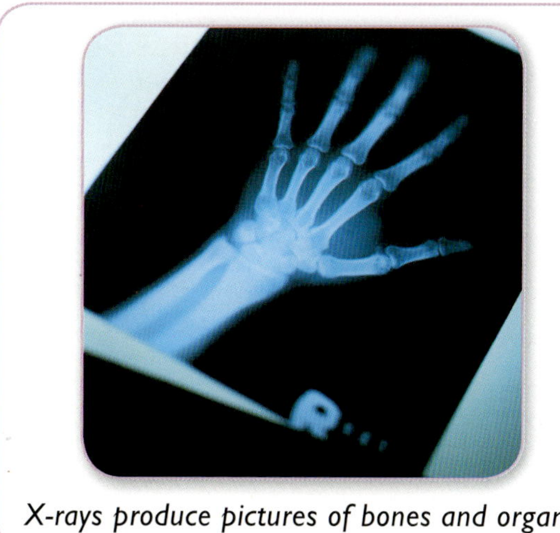

X-rays produce pictures of bones and organs.

Radiology

Radiology is a medicinal science that helps in the early diagnosis and treatment of diseases. Radiologists can see the inside of the human body by using radiology equipment like X-ray machines. Modern radiological procedures can even produce moving and three-dimensional images of organs.

Nuclear Physics

Nuclear physics studies the atomic nuclei. It studies the structure and various properties of the atomic nuclei and their reactions. Nuclear physics has created new techniques for diagnosing and treating disease, developing nuclear weapons, sterilizing and preserving food, exploring oil, and monitoring environmental pollution. It is also used in the field of astrophysics, biochemistry and chemistry.

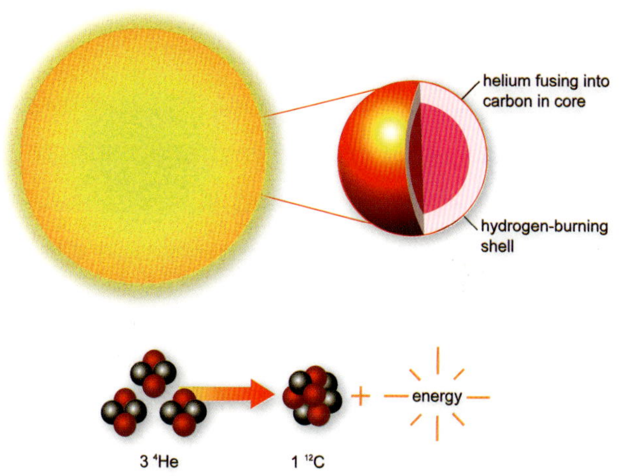

Nuclear fusion is a process in which two nuclei combine to release large amounts of energy.

Name of Science	Subject
Aerology	the study of the free atmosphere
Biometeorology	the study of the effects of atmospheric conditions on living organisms
Cynology	the study of dogs
Dendrology	the study of trees
Entomology	the study of insects
Exobiology	the study of life in outer space
Gerontology	the study of old age
Heliology	the study of the Sun
Ichthyology	the study of fish
Japanology	the study of Japanese culture
Kymatology	the study of waves or wave motions

Name of Science	Subject
Lithology	the study of rocks
Myrmecology	the study of ants
Nosology	the study of diseases
Oology	the study of eggs
Pyrology	the study of fire
Rheology	the study of flow
Selenology	the study of the moon
Toxicology	the study of poisons
Urology	the study and treatment of diseases of the urogenital tract
Vexillology	the study of flags
Xylology	the study of wood
Zymology	the study of fermentation

What is Force?

Force is a push or pull. Forces are all around us. Daily life actions such as opening doors, lifting bags, stretching, bending, walking, and running require the use of force. When force is applied to an object, it produces motion and the object moves. Without force, nothing can move or stop.

Objects start to move or come to rest only when a force is applied.

Friction

Friction is a force that resists the motion of an object. Friction is the resistance produced between two surfaces in contact with each other. Friction can be reduced or increased. Oil is used to reduce friction between rotating devices.

A road and a car tyre have friction between them.

Upthrust

A force that pushes an object upwards in a fluid or gas is called upthrust. It is also called buoyancy. Buoyancy keeps an object floating in water. Swimmers remain on the water surface due to upthrust.

The forces acting on this glass are balanced. This keeps the glass from toppling over.

Balanced Forces

Forces can be balanced or unbalanced. When objects do not move, there is a balanced force. Balanced forces are opposite in direction and equal. They do not cause change in motion. For example, a glass on a table does not move because both the forces, the force of gravity acting downward and the force from the surface pushing it up, are balanced.

Unbalanced Forces

Unbalanced forces cause change in motion. They are unequal and are not opposite like balanced forces.

Speed and Velocity

Speed is the distance travelled by an object in a unit time. For example, a bike traveling at a speed of 40 km/h will travel a distance of 40 km in an hour. Velocity is the speed of an object along with the direction of its motion.

Pressure

Pressure is the force that acts on a unit area of surface. A thin surface object exerts more pressure than a wide surface object. For example, a knife can easily cut an object because of its thin and sharp surface.

Quick Look

Acceleration is the rate at which the velocity of an object changes. Objects that are changing their speed or their direction are said to be accelerating.

Seesaw is an example of unbalanced forces.

Cars move at high speeds in a race.

A fork and knife uses pressure to pick and cut food.

Newton's Laws of Motion

Isaac Newton described the three *laws of motion* to describe motions both on earth and space.

First Law – An object in a state of uniform motion remain in that state of motion unless an external force is applied to it.

Second Law – The net force on an object is equal to the mass of the object multiplied by its acceleration.

Third Law – To every action there is an opposite and equal reaction.

What is weight?

Weight is a vertical force exerted on an object because of gravity. Gravity attracts an object towards the earth. The weight of an object depends on both the amount of mass and the amount of gravity acting on it. Therefore, a place with less gravity would cause an object to have less weight.

What is mass?

Mass is the amount of matter in an object. Mass never changes and always remains the same. Mass does not change with the location of an object. Therefore, the mass of an object will remain the same on earth or anywhere in the universe.

Balance

A balance is a pair of scales or weighing pans. It is used to measure the weight or mass of an object. A balance compares an unknown amount of matter to a standard weight using a lever balance.

Spring Scale

A spring scale measures the weight of an object by the distance a spring deflects under its load. Spring scales are always calibrated to read the weight an object.

A heavier object moves lower in the balance, while a lighter object moves higher.

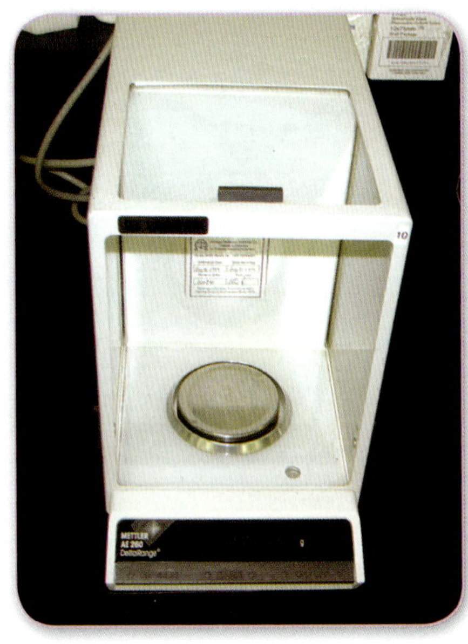

A Mettler digital analytical balance with a precision of up to 0.1mg.

Typical Weights

An average man:	70 kilograms
An average woman:	60 kilograms
A new born baby:	2.6 kilograms
A small car:	650 kilograms
A cell phone:	90 to 125 grams

As a baby grows, it gains weight.

Name of Unit	Symbol	Equivalent	Typical Item Measured In This Unit
microgram	µg	0.000 001 g	medicine
milligram	mg	1000 µg	medicine
gram	g	1000 mg	small amounts of food or jewellery
kilogram	kg	1000 g	body mass, weight of furniture and large objects, bag of rice, wheat, vegetables
ton	t	1000 kg	weights of cars, boats, ships, large animals
megagram	Mg	1 ton	rarely used, as ton is preferred
megaton	Mt	1 million tons	megaton is not actually used, in measuring common things.

Weight on Earth and Moon

The weight of an object on the moon's surface is about 1/6th of the weight of the same object on the earth's surface. For example, a man weighing 54 kg on earth will weigh only 9 kg on the moon.

Units of Weight and Mass

The SI unit of mass is *kilogram*. It is almost universally used as the standard unit of mass. Newton is the associated SI unit of force and weight. In the United States common units, *pound* is the unit of force and weight.

A precision balance scale for weighing silver and gold located on display at the Historic Archive and Museum of Mining in Pachuca, Mexico.

A human will weigh less on the moon.

A calibrated home weighing machine.

Quick Look

Newton's second law is used for weight and mass conversions. The acceleration due to gravity on earth is 9.8 m/s^2. To convert mass into weight, multiply the mass by 9.8. To convert weight into mass, divide the weight by 9.8.

What is light?

Light is a form of energy. We see everything around us because of light. Sun is the biggest source of natural light. Other sources of light are artificial, such as, lamps, electric bulbs, tube lights, etc.

Sunlight travels at about 300,000 kilometres per second.

Speed of Light

Light travels at a constant speed of 299,792,458 m/s. Sunlight reaches the earth in just 8 minutes and travels about 1,48,864,320 kilometres from the sun.

Implying light using natural or artificial sources is known as illumination.

White Light

White light is the light that comes from the sun or light bulbs. The white light is actually a mixture of many different colours. We can see the colours of white light by scattering it through a prism.

Shadow

A shadow forms when an object blocks the way of light. Any opaque object that blocks light will cast a shadow. The size of the shadow depends upon the distance of light from the object and size of the object.

If the sun is shining behind an object, its shadow will form in front.

Shadows of trees at sunset.

Changing Shadows

During the day, the length of a shadow changes. Shadows can be extremely long during sunrise and sunset. At noon, when the sun is directly overhead, it does not cast any shadow.

Quick Look

Optics is a branch of physics that deals with the scientific study of light. It studies the behaviour and properties of light.

Eclipse

Eclipses are celestial events that occur because of shadows formed in space. During an eclipse, one celestial object blocks the path of light of another object. When earth blocks the sunlight on moon, lunar eclipse occurs and when moon blocks sunlight, casting a shadow on the earth, solar eclipse occurs.

Transparent, Translucent and Opaque

Light passes through materials or gets absorbed in some objects. The objects which let the light pass through them are called transparent materials. Glass, air and water are transparent materials. Plastics and clothes are translucent materials that let some of the light pass through them. Most of the other materials like metal, wood and stone are opaque materials that absorb much of the energy and do not let the light pass through them.

Every 15 minutes the sun produces enough power to supply the earth for an entire year.

Solar eclipse forming a diamond ring.

Lemon and candle stand present inside the transparent glass are clearly visible.

Types of Sources of Light

Natural: sunlight, meteors/meteor showers, stars, lighting

Direct Chemical: chemoluminescence, fluorescence, phosphorescence

Combustion-based: candles, fire, gas lighting, kerosene lamps, lanterns, oil lamps

 Reflection of Light

The bouncing back of light from a surface is called reflection. Light always reflects back from a surface at the same angle it hits the surface. The ray of light which hits the surface is called the incident ray and reflected ray is the ray of light which leaves the surface. Mirror, surface of water and plate glass are best materials that reflect light.

Water reflecting sunlight.

 Refraction of Light

The process of bending of light when it passes from one medium to another is called refraction. Light travels in a straight line through air. But when it travels from one medium to another, it changes direction. When light enters water, it slows down, changes direction and bends slightly.

 Prism

A prism is a triangular-shaped glass through which light can bend. When white light passes through a prism, it splits into different colours. The prism is used in laboratories to demonstrate that light is composed of different colours.

Prism diverges white light into a rainbow pattern.

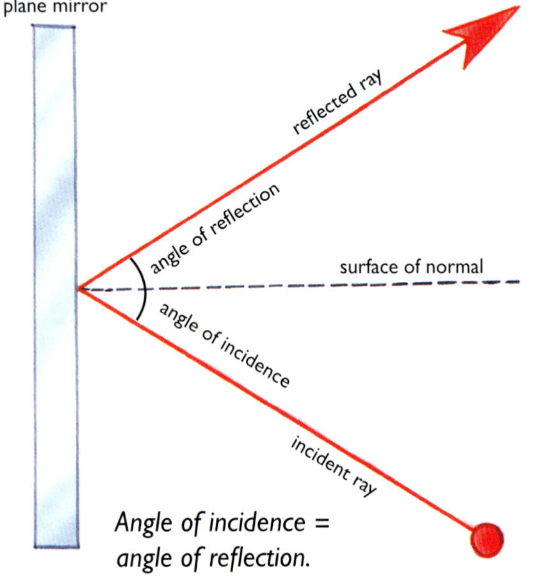

Angle of incidence = angle of reflection.

Law of Reflection

When a ray of light strikes the surface of a mirror, it is reflected back. The incident ray and the reflected ray make the same angle with respect to the surface normal. According to the law of reflection, the angle of incidence – the angle formed between the normal and the incident ray is equal to the angle of reflection – the angle formed between the normal and the reflected ray.

Rainbow

Rainbow is a colourful arc in the sky that forms when the sun shines during or shortly after a shower of rain. Rainbows are caused by the refraction of light through water droplets in the air. Each water droplet acts as a prism and splits sunlight into its seven component colours.

Rainbow Colours

Violet, indigo, blue, green, yellow, orange and red are the seven colours of a rainbow. The colours of rainbow can be remembered by memorising the word VIBGYOR.

Light Absorption

A light beam is reflected and diffused when it falls on a bright object. When light falls on a dark or black object, most of it is absorbed and very little light is reflected back.

Diffraction

Diffraction is the process of bending or spreading of light when it passes through an opening or an edge. A diffracted light spreads out in all directions.

Quick Look

Optical fibers are thin, thread-like fibers made of glass or plastic. They are used to transmit information as light pulses. Optical fibers are widely used in telecommunications.

The centre of a rainbow's arc is directly opposite the sun.

A black suitcase absorbs all light and reflects little or none.

A pencil submerged in water appears bent because light rays passing from air through water bend or change their direction because of refraction.

Heat and Energy

Heat is a form of energy. Heat makes things hot by adding energy. Energy is the ability to do work. Nothing is possible without energy. The food we eat contains energy. We use that energy to speak, move, see, think and to perform other activities.

Heat Transfer

Heat moves in three different ways: conduction, convection and radiation. Conduction is the transfer of heat energy from one material to another through direct physical contact. Convection is heat transfer in gases or liquids. Radiation is the third form of heat transfer. The sun's heat energy reaches the earth by radiation. Radiation is a type of heat transfer that does not need a medium. So, heat from the sun can travel through the vacuum of space to reach the earth.

Temperature and Thermometer

The measurement of the hotness or coldness of a body is called its temperature. Temperature is measured in units called degrees. Thermometer is the instrument used to measure temperature. There are many types of thermometers. Mercury and alcohol thermometers are the most common. Thermometers are usually calibrated in degrees of Fahrenheit or Celsius.

Quick Look

Joule is the SI unit of energy.
One Joule is equal to 0.2390 calories.

Biomass is renewable organic material such as wood, grasses and crops that can be converted into fuel.

The heat from the fire gets transferred and boils the water.

Wind energy comes from moving air which is converted to electric power to create electricity.

Forms of Energy

Energy can change from one form to another but cannot be created or destroyed. Chemical energy, nuclear energy, light energy, heat energy, electric energy, and gravitational energy are different forms of energy. Heat energy keeps us warm while light and sound energy help us to see and hear.

Stationary balloons have potential energy in them.

Kinetic and Potential Energy

Kinetic energy is the energy that a body has as a result of its motion. All moving objects have kinetic energy. Potential energy is the energy stored in a body. Potential energy can be converted into kinetic energy. Electrical energy, radiant energy, thermal energy, sound and motion energy are several forms of kinetic energy. Potential energy also has different forms including chemical energy, nuclear energy, and gravitational energy.

A girl riding a cycle is an example of kinetic energy.

Renewable and Non-renewable Energy

Renewable energy is energy derived from natural resources that are constantly being replenished by nature and will never get exhausted. Non-renewable energy is obtained from resources that cannot be replenished when used once.

Solar thermal power plant uses solar energy.

Sources of Energy

Renewable Energy	Non-renewable Energy
Solar Energy	Oil
Wind Energy	Natural Gas
Geothermal Energy	Coal
Hydropower Energy	Nuclear Energy
Biomass	Uranium
Ocean Energy	Propane

What is electricity and magnetism?

Electricity is a type of energy. It is the flow of electric power or charge through a conductor. Electricity is used to operate television, computers, and radio. Electricity is generated at power stations. Magnetism is a physical property of some solids that attracts or repels other materials. Magnetism makes some metal objects spin or stick to other metals.

Static Electricity

Static electricity is the electric charge generated by friction between two objects. Rubbing two different materials together like wool on plastic or the soles of shoes on the carpet produces static electricity. Flyaway hair is one of the common examples of static electricity.

Quick Look

William Gilbert founded the sciences of electricity and magnetism and the relationship between them. He described his ideas in a book called *De Magnete* in 1600.

Ammeter is an instrument that measures electric current in amperes.

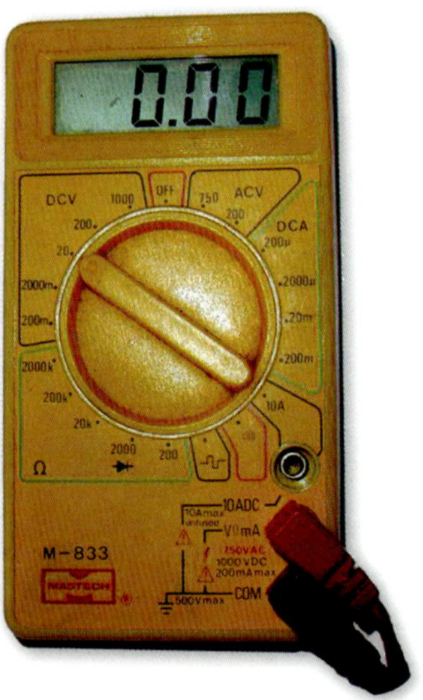

Voltmeter is an electric device that measures voltage flowing through a circuit.

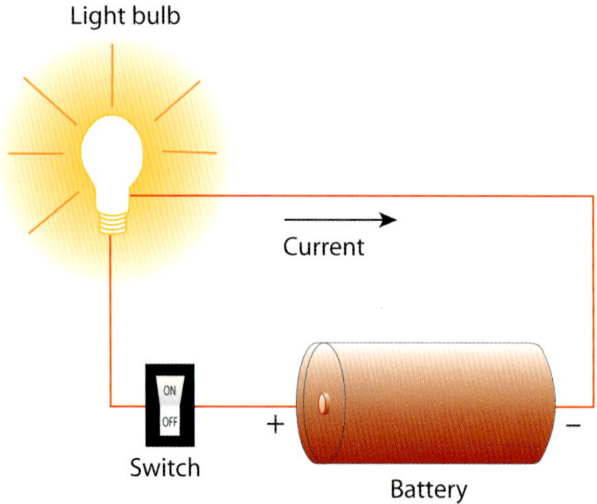

Diagram of a simple circuit.

Current Electricity

Current electricity is electricity that travels through a circuit. It is the continuous movement of charged particles along a path or wire. Current electricity is used as a source of energy in homes and industries.

Conductors and Insulators

Conductors are substances that allow electricity to flow through them easily. Insulators are substances that do not allow electricity to flow through them.

Magnet

Magnets are materials that can attract or repel other magnets or metals. Iron, steel, nickel, cobalt are some metals that can be easily attracted by a magnet. Magnets can be of different shapes and sizes. Some magnets are U-shaped and therefore called horseshoe magnets, while long and straight magnets are called bar magnets.

Magnetic Field

Magnetic field is the area surrounding a magnet in which other magnetic objects can be affected by its magnetism. Imaginary magnetic lines are used to represent the magnetic field of a magnet. The stronger a magnet the larger will be its magnetic field.

North Pole and South Pole

All magnets have two ends: north and south. The north end is called the north pole and the south end is called the south pole. Opposite poles of two magnets attract each other and similar poles repel each other.

Lodestone

Lodestone is a natural magnetic rock. It is made up of magnetite, a form of iron oxide. Lodestone can attract and magnetise iron.

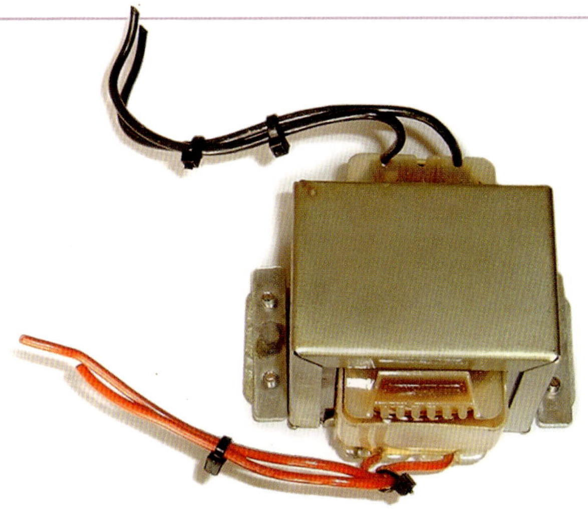

Transformer is an electric device used to increase and decrease voltage and current.

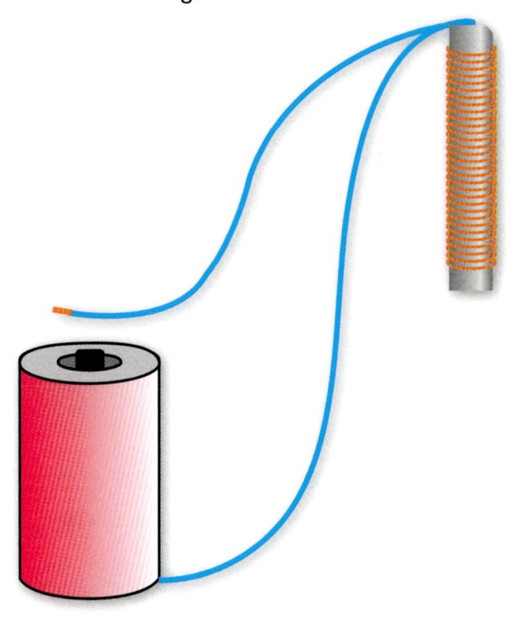

Temporary magnets show magnetic properties only when exposed to an external magnetic field.

The name "magnet" comes from lodestones found in Magnesia, Greece.

 What is sound?

Sound is a form of energy. Sound is produced by vibration of materials. These vibrations travel through the air in the form of sound waves and enter our ears. Sound travels through solid, liquids and gases but cannot travel through vacuum.

Our ears help us hear sound.

 Speed of Sound

Speed of sound depends on the type of medium and the temperature of the medium through which it passes. Sound travels faster in solids and liquids than in gases. Sound travels at a speed of 5,950 metres per second through iron, 1,497 metres per second through distilled water and 316 metres per second through oxygen.

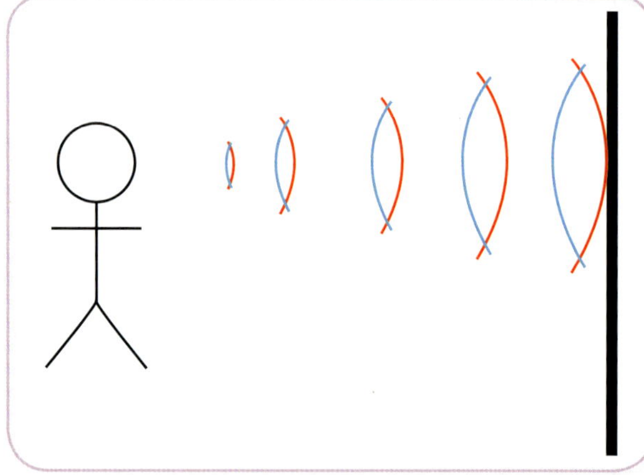

Schematic diagram of echo showing the bouncing back of sound waves.

 Echo

Reflected sound is called an echo. Echoes and original sounds can be heard separately. Echoes can be heard at the bottom of a well, in large halls, caves and even in between hills or mountains. Chorusing is a long echo, while phasing is a short type of echo.

String Musical Instruments

String musical instruments use strings to produce musical notes. The vibration of strings produce sound. Guitar, violin, and mandolin are some examples of string musical instruments.

Banjo is a stringed musical instrument developed by African slaves in the United States.

Wind Musical Instruments

Wind musical instruments produce sound by the vibration of a column of air. The column of air vibrates when wind is blown into or across the instrument. Wind instruments are also known as aerophones. Flute, harmonica, saxophone, and crumhorn are some examples of wind musical instruments.

Brass Musical Instruments

Brass musical instruments are made of brass and have cup-shaped mouthpieces without reeds. The instruments are played by blowing air through the mouthpieces. Trumpet, horn, trombone and tuba are brass musical instruments.

Keyboard Musical Instruments

Piano, carillon, pipe organ, clavichord, and mellotron are keyboard musical instruments. Keyboard instruments are played by striking individual keys. Each key produces one or more sound.

Percussion Musical Instruments

Musical instruments that create sound by striking and shaking are called percussion instruments. They are the world's oldest musical instruments. Percussion musical instruments are drums, timpani, cymbals, gong, xylophone etc.

Flutes usually have three to eight finger holes.

Trumpet is a popular brass musical instrument.

Piano is the most common keyboard musical instrument.

Quick Look

Acoustics is the scientific study of sound and sound waves.

Electronic Musical Instruments

Electronic musical instruments produces sound using electronics. Electronic musical instruments include the Hammond organ, MIDI, synthesizer, and mini GEM.

What is gravitation?

Gravitation is the force of attraction between all objects in the universe. The strength of gravitation between two objects depends on their masses. Larger the object more will be the gravitational force between them.

Newton's Law of Universal Gravitation

The English scientist, Isaac Newton devised the Law of Universal Gravitation. Newton stated that every object in the universe exerts a force of attraction on other objects. This force is known as the gravitational force. The force of attraction increases with the increase in the masses of the objects and decreases with the increase in the distance between the objects. The direction of the gravitational force is along the line joining the objects.

Earth's Gravity

Gravity on earth is the force that tends to pull all objects towards the centre of the earth. It is denoted by 'g' and its approximate value is 9.8 m/s^2. It is because of gravity that all objects on the earth have weight.

Free Fall

Free fall happens when an object falls under the force of gravity alone. Usually, free fall does not occur on the earth as air resistance opposes the gravitational pull acting on the falling object.

Gravitational force keeps the earth and the other planets in their orbits around the sun.

The Earth's gravitational attraction is maximum at the surface.

Skydivers in free fall.

Effects of Gravitation on Earth

Gravitational force is responsible for various natural phenomena occurring on the earth. The gravitational pull of the earth on all objects holds all objects to the surface of the earth. Ocean tides are caused by the gravitational attraction between the oceans and the moon or the sun. Gravitation is also responsible for the existence of the atmosphere around the earth.

The apple falls directly down to the earth because of gravity.

Weightlessness

An object becomes weightless when little or no gravity acts on it. For example, when a spacecraft orbits around the earth, it constantly accelerates towards the earth. The spacecraft occupants are in a free fall state as the earth's weak gravitational force is cancelled out by the earth's gravitational field. The free fall state creates a condition of weightlessness in the spacecraft.

Astronauts in the state of weightlessness.

Centre of Gravity

Centre of gravity is an imaginary point in an object where the total weight of the body may be thought to be concentrated. In other words, it is the point in an object where the force of gravity appears to act. The concept of centre of gravity is used in many day to day life applications.

Engineers build cars and aeroplanes using the concept of centre of gravity.

Quick Look

You weigh slightly less when the moon is directly overhead due to gravitational effects.

What is an atom?

An atom is the smallest and basic unit of the simplest substance, a chemical element. An atom has all the characteristics of the element. Atom is made up of three basic particles: protons, neutrons and electrons. Everything around us is made up of atoms.

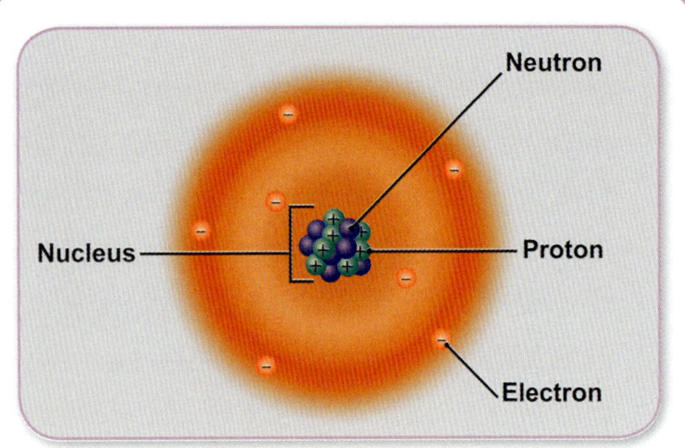

The smallest atom has only a single proton.

Atom Structure

All atoms have a nucleus in the centre around which negatively charged electrons orbit. Both the protons and neutrons reside in the nucleus. Protons have a positive charge, while neutrons have no charge so they are neutral.

Atomic Number and Mass Number

The number of protons present in an atom determines the atomic number of the atom. As the mass of the electron is very small, so the protons and neutrons make up most of the atomic mass. Mass number is the sum of neutrons and protons. The number of protons in an element is constant but the number of neutrons may vary, so atomic mass number may also vary.

The atomic mass number is different for different isotopes of the same element.

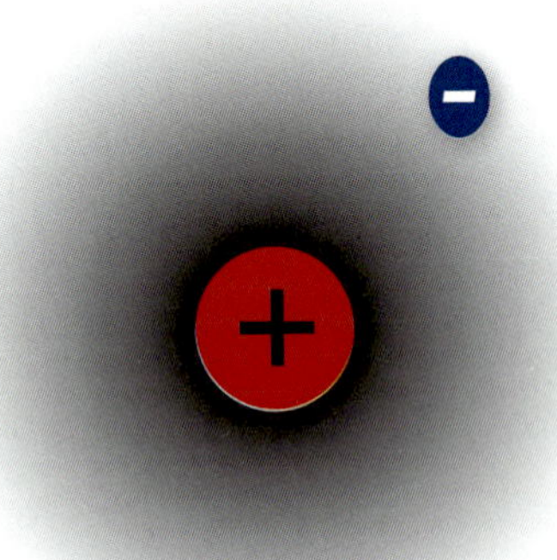

Protium is the most common isotope of hydrogen. It has one proton and one electron but no neutrons.

Isotopes

Atoms that have same number of protons but different number of neutrons are known as isotopes. Many elements that exist in nature have more than one isotope. For example, hydrogen has three naturally occurring isotopes. They have neutrons, protons and electrons in them but the most commonly existing isotope has no neutrons. The other two isotopes have one or two neutrons in addition to one proton.

John Dalton

In 1803, John Dalton proposed his atomic theory in which he stated that atoms were indivisible and could be neither created nor destroyed. Dalton also stated that atoms of an element are identical in their size, shape and mass. According to his theory, when atoms combine to form a particular compound, they always do so in a specific numeric ratio.

John Dalton was a British scientist.

Radioactivity

Radioactivity is the constant emission of radiations from an atom. Radioactive atoms have an unstable nucleus that spontaneously changes into the nucleus of another isotope. Such atoms emit energy in the form of particles or electromagnetic waves. The most common types of radiation are alpha, beta and gamma radiations. Atoms of radium and uranium are radioactive.

Henri Becquerel discovered radioactivity in 1896.

Nuclear Fission

Nuclear fission is the splitting of a heavy nucleus into two or more smaller nuclei. The process gives out large amount of energy and free neutrons. Nuclear reactors produce energy by the process of nuclear fission.

Quick Look

The word "atom" is a Greek word that means indivisible.

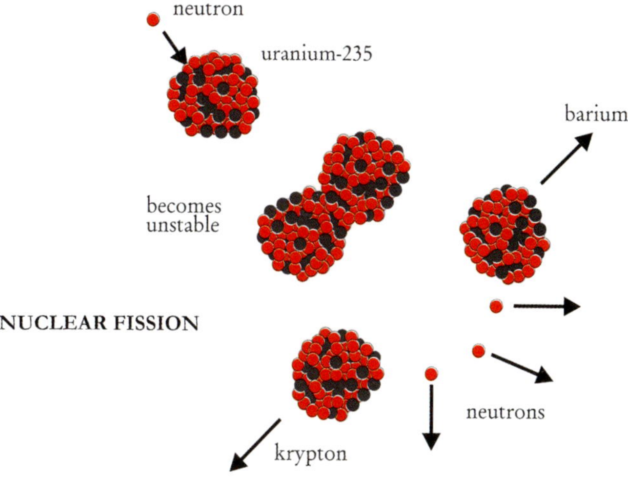

Uranium is the main element used in nuclear reactors and atomic bombs.

What is an element?

An element is a pure chemical substance composed of identical atoms. An element cannot be broken down further into any simpler substance. The atoms of an element always have the same atomic number, which means that all atoms have same number of protons.

Dmitri Ivanovich Mendeleev

Dmitri Ivanovich Mendeleev was a 19th century chemist who is credited with the creation of the first version of the periodic table. Using the table, he was able to predict the properties of elements that were yet to be discovered.

John Alexander Reina Newlands

John Alexander Reina Newlands was an analytical chemist who prepared the first periodic table in 1863. In his periodic table, Newlands arranged the elements in order of their relative atomic masses.

Nitrogen

Nitrogen is a chemical element that exists as a colourless, odourless inert diatomic gas. It was discovered in 1772 by Daniel Rutherford, a Scottish physician. Nitrogen constitutes 78% by volume of the earth's atmosphere.

Quick Look

A small group of elements that exhibits properties of both metals and nonmetals is known as metalloid group.

Dmitri Ivanovich Mendeleev was a Russian chemist.

John Alexander Reina Newlands was an English chemist.

Halogens

The elements in the seventh group of the periodic table are called halogens. Examples of halogens are fluorine, chlorine, bromine, iodine, etc. The top most halogen is the most chemically active and as we move downwards in the group, the chemical activity of the halogen decreases. Halogens are poisonous in nature. For example, chlorine gas and chlorine compounds are used as chemical weapons.

Element Symbols

Elements are known by common names as well as by their abbreviations. These abbreviations consist of one or two letters, with the first letter capitalized. These abbreviations are called element symbols. They are mostly derived from English, Latin or German words. For example, the symbols of some common elements are:

Carbon	C
Zinc	Zn
Calcium	Ca
Oxygen	O
Radium	Ra

Oxygen

Oxygen is the third most abundant chemical element in the universe, after hydrogen and helium. It is represented by the symbol O. It is the most abundant element to exist in the earth's crust. Oxygen is present in our biosphere, sea, land and air. Oxygen occurs in three isotopes, ^{16}O, ^{17}O and ^{18}O.

Periodic Table

Periodic table is an arrangement of chemical elements in a tabular manner. The elements in the periodic table are categorised on the basis of their atomic numbers and similarity of properties.

PERIODIC TABLE

hydrogen 1 H 1.0079																		helium 2 He 4.0026
lithium 3 Li 6.941	berylium 4 Be 9.0122												boron 5 B 10.811	carbon 6 C 12.011	nitrogen 7 N 14.007	oxygen 8 O 15.999	fluorine 9 F 18.998	neon 10 Ne 20.180
sodium 11 Na 22.990	magnesium 12 Mg 24.305												aluminium 13 Al 26.982	silicon 14 Si 28.086	phosphorus 15 P 30.974	sulfur 16 S 32.065	chlorine 17 Cl 35.453	argon 18 Ar 39.348
potassium 19 K 39.098	calcium 20 Ca 40.078		scandium 21 Sc 44.956	titanium 22 Ti 47.867	vanadium 23 V 44.956	chromium 24 Cr 47.867	manganese 25 Mn 54.938	iron 26 Fe 55.845	cobalt 27 Co 58.845	nickel 28 Ni 58.693	copper 29 Cu 63.546	zinc 30 Zn 65.39	gallium 31 Ga 69.723	germanium 32 Ge 72.61	arsenic 33 As 74.922	selenium 34 Se 78.96	bromine 35 Br 79.904	krypton 36 Kr 83.08
rubidium 37 Rb 85.468	calcium 38 Sr 87.62		yttrium 39 Y 88.906	zirconium 40 Zr 91.224	niobium 41 Nb 92.906	molybdenum 42 Mo 95.94	technetium 43 Tc [98]	ruthenium 44 Ru 102.91	rhodium 45 Rh 101.07	palladium 46 Pd 106.42	silver 47 Ag 107.87	cadmium 48 Cd 112.41	indium 49 In 131.29	tin 50 Sn 131.29	antimony 51 Sb 131.29	tellurium 52 Te 131.29	iodine 53 I 131.29	xenon 54 Xe 131.29
caesium 55 Cs 132.91	barium 56 Ba 137.33	57-70 *	lutelium 71 Lu 174.97	hafnium 72 Hf 178.49	tantalum 73 Ta 180.95	tungsten 74 W 183.84	rhenium 75 Re 186.21	osmium 76 Os 192.22	iridium 77 Ir 190.23	platinum 78 Pt 195.08	gold 79 Au 196.97	mercury 80 Hg 200.59	thallium 81 Tl 204.38	lead 82 Pb 207.2	bismuth 83 Bi 208.98	polonium 84 Po [209]	astatine 85 At [210]	radon 86 Rn [222]
francium 87 Fr [223]	radium 88 Ra [226]	89-102 **	lawrencium 103 Lr [262]	rutherfordium 104 Rf [261]	dubnium 105 Db [262]	seaborgium 106 Sg [266]	bohriuium 107 Bh [264]	hassium 108 Hs [269]	meitnerium 109 Mt [268]	ununnilium 110 Uun [271]	unununium 111 Uuu [272]	ununbium 112 Uub [277]		ununquadium 114 Uuq [289]				

* Lanthanide series	lanthanum 57 La 138.91	cerium 58 Ce 140.12	praseodymium 59 Pr 140.91	neodymium 60 Nd 144.24	promethium 61 Pm [145]	samarium 62 Sm 150.36	europium 63 Eu 151.96	gadolinium 64 Gd 157.25	terbium 65 Tb 158.93	dysprosium 66 Dy 162.50	holmium 67 Ho 164.93	rebium 68 Er 167.26	thulium 69 Tm 168.93	ytterbium 70 Yb 173.04
** Actinide series	actinium 89 Ac [227]	thorium 90 Th 232.04	protactinium 91 Pa 231.04	uranium 92 U 238.03	neptunium 93 Np [237]	plutonium 94 Pu [244]	americium 95 Am [243]	cerium 96 Cm [247]	berkelium 97 Bk [247]	californium 98 Cf [251]	elnsleinium 99 Es [252]	fermium 100 Fm [257]	mendelevium 101 Md [258]	nobelium 102 No [259]

The horizontal rows of elements form a period and the vertical ones form a group. Elements falling under the same group show similar chemical properties.

What are metals?

Metals are elements that form a large part of our earth. Metals have a shiny appearance and most have high density. They are also very good conductors of heat and electricity. All metals except mercury are solid at room temperature.

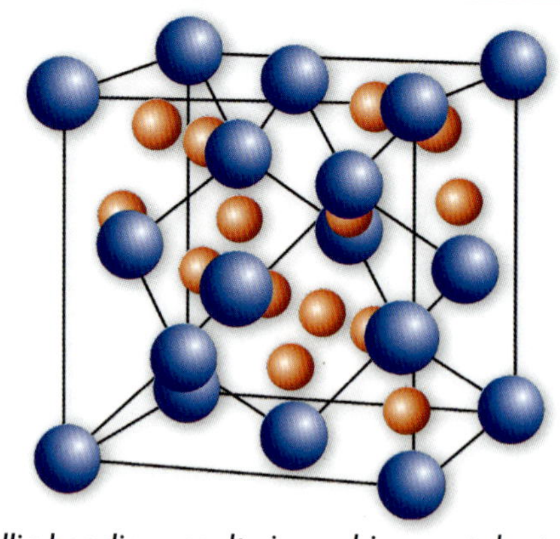

Metallic bonding results in making metals strong, malleable and good conductors of heat.

Valuable Elements

Metals have high tensile strength and are capable of being molded into different shapes on heating and melting. Therefore, metals are used to make large structures and buildings. All bridges, ships, aeroplanes, machineries, pipelines, electric wires are made using metals such as iron, silver, etc. Metals like silver, copper and gold are used to make coins and medals. They are also useful in making jewelry.

Gold is used to make coins.

Brass is an alloy that is used to make tough and durable objects like bells.

What are alloys?

An alloy is a substance produced by the combination of two or more metals. Some strong metals are mixed with other less valuable metals to enhance their qualities. For example, a poor metal, like tin, is mixed with copper to form a dense and heavy alloy, bronze. Alloys are also formed by mixing a metal and a non metal. For example, steel is an alloy of iron mixed with small amounts of carbon.

Alloy	Composition
Duralumin	93.5% aluminum, 4.4% copper, 1.5% magnesium and 0.6% manganese
Brass	varied proportions of copper and zinc
Stainless steel	88% iron, 10% chromium, 2% carbon
Copper amalgam	70% mercury and 30% copper
German silver	65% copper, 18% nickel and 17% zinc
Britannia metal	93% tin, 5% antimony and 2% copper

TYPES OF METALS	LOCATION IN THE PERIODIC TABLE	CHARACTERISTICS	EXAMPLES
Alkali metals	Group I A	Soft, have low melting points and densities.	Lithium, sodium, potassium, rubidium
Alkaline-earth metals	Group II A	Very soft, react readily with water.	Beryllium, magnesium, calcium, strontium
Rare-earth metals	Group III B	Shiny, burn in air, have high melting and boiling points.	Lanthanides, yttrium, scandium
Transition metals	Elements from Groups 3 to 12. d-block elements.	Exhibit magnetic properties, high density, high melting and boiling points.	Titanium, chromium, iron, copper

Metallography

Metallography is a science dealing with the constitution and structure of metals and alloys. People who practice metallography are known as metallographers. Metallographers study metals and alloys using optical microscope, electron microscope and x-rays. They determine how materials will react under certain conditions.

Pliers are usually made of steel alloys with additives such as Vanadium and Chromium.

Quick Look

Extractive metallurgy is the science of extracting valuable metals from their ores and refining the extracted metal to a pure form.

Metallic Facts

Most tensile metals:	Copper, Iron and Platinum
Most malleable metals:	Gold, Silver, Copper, Tin and Aluminum
Hardest metal:	Chromium
Softest metal:	Cesium
Most dense metals:	Osmium, Iridium, Platinum, Gold, Tungsten
Best conductors of electricity:	Silver, Copper, Gold and Aluminum
Radioactive metals:	Uranium, Plutonium, Radium.

What are states of matter?

Matter exists in different states. Solids, liquids, and gases are the three states of matter. All states of matter are made up of tiny particles, which differ in nature and arrangement.

What is a solid?

Solid is a state of matter that has a fixed shape and volume. All the particles in a solid are held close together and arranged in a regular pattern. These particles can only vibrate but cannot move freely.

Ice is a solid substance.

What is a liquid?

Liquid is a state of matter that has a fixed volume but not any fixed shape. Liquids can change their shape according to the shape of the container in which they are kept. The particles inside a liquid can move around each other easily as they have no regular arrangement. Water is a liquid.

Liquids take the shape of a glass when poured into it.

Steam is a gaseous form of water.

What is a gas?

Gas is a state of matter that does not have a fixed shape or volume. The particles inside a gaseous substance move rapidly. They have large spaces between them and have no regular arrangement. Water vapour, hydrogen, nitrogen and oxygen are examples of gas.

Processes of Changing States		
Condensation	gas to liquid	gas cools and changes state
Freezing	liquid to solid	liquid cools and changes state
Sublimation	solid to gas	changes state directly
Evaporation	liquid to gas	increase in temperature changes state
Melting	solid to liquid	increase in temperature changes state
Frost formation	gas to solid	gas directly changes to solid

Water

Water is the only substance that can go through all the states of matter without changing its chemical properties. Water usually exists as a liquid. Water freezes at a temperature of 0°C and changes into its solid state called ice. Water turns into gas or water vapour when heated. Most of the water on the earth's surface exists in a liquid or solid state. Water can also be found in the atmosphere as vapour.

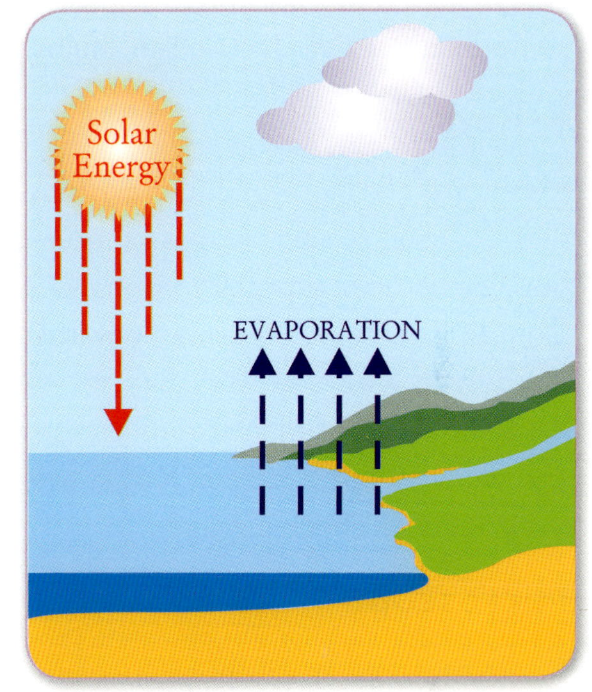

At higher temperatures, the number of energetic molecules is greater, and evapouration is more rapid.

Condensation

Condensation is the process of changing water from its gaseous state into liquid state. Condensation generally occurs in the atmosphere when warm air rises and cools down. For example, a glass full of ice will have water droplets outside it. These droplets appear as a result of the cooling down of the air present in atmosphere.

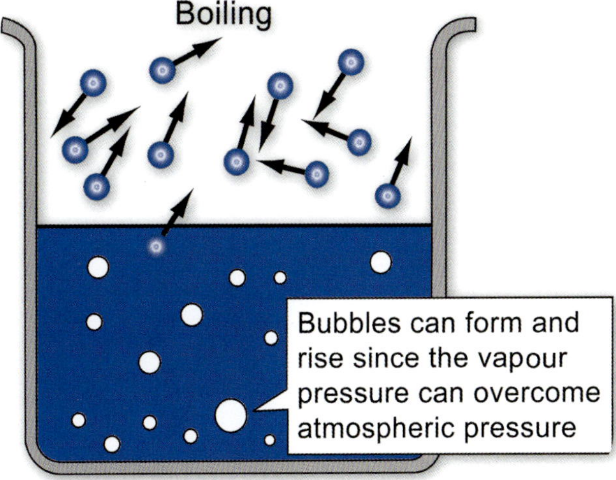

Boiling point is a temperature at which a liquid changes into a vapour.

Quick Look

Glass is solid but has the molecular structure of a liquid. It is made by melting silica, potash or lead oxide at high temperatures.

 Light Bulb

The light bulb was invented by Thomas Alva Edison. A light bulb is a glass bulb containing a wire filament that produces light when electricity passes through it. Compact fluorescent lamps, tube-style fluorescent lamps, mercury vapour lamps and ultraviolet lamps are some examples of electric light bulbs.

Electric light bulb was invented, in December 1879.

 X-Rays

X-rays are electromagnetic radiations that are used to take images of internal body structures, especially bones. Wilhelm Conrad Roentgen, a German physicist discovered X-rays in 1895. Besides medicine, X-rays are also used in scientific research and industry. For example, X-rays are used in airports to check luggage.

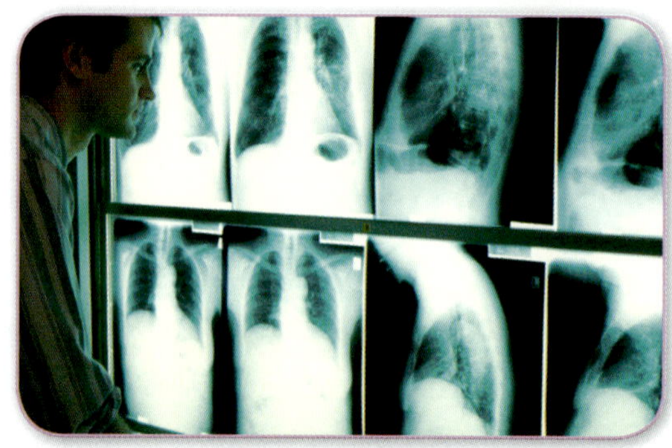

X-rays have smaller wavelengths and therefore higher energy than ultraviolet waves.

 Microscope

The microscope is an optical instrument used for observing very small objects. Antony van Leeuwenhoek is known as the "Father of Microscopy" because he was the first person to use a simple microscope to observe blood, insects and many other objects.

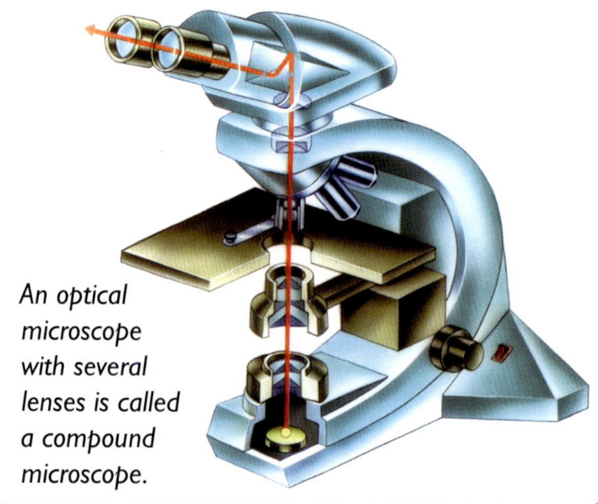

An optical microscope with several lenses is called a compound microscope.

Types of Microscope

Microscope	Description
Compound Microscope	It is a light microscope that consists of two lenses. It is a commonly used microscope.
Dissection Microscope	It is used in science laboratories for dissecting animals. It is also known as stereo microscope.
Scanning Electron Microscope (SEM)	It is an electron microscope that can magnify as much as 300, 000 times.
Transmission Electron Microscope (TEM)	It gives a 2-dimensional view. Electron beams pass through this microscope.

Penicillin

Penicillin is the most well-known drug used to treat infections. Penicillin is used to treat different kinds of infections including skin, dental, ear, respiratory tract and urinary tract infection. Sir Alexander Fleming, a British biologist, discovered penicillin in 1928.

Telescope

Thetelescope is an optical device designed to see distant objects. Galileo Galilei was the first to use a telescope to explore the universe in 1609. There are two types of telescopes, refractor telescope and reflector telescope. Refractor telescopes are very large and use lenses, while reflector telescopes use mirrors.

Radium

Radium is a silvery-white, radioactive element. The symbol of Radium is Ra and its atomic number is 88. Radium was discovered by Marie Curie and Pierre Curie in 1898. Radium is used in the treatment of some kinds of cancer.

Thermometer

The thermometer is an instrument used to measure temperature. The word thermometer is made up of two smaller words: *thermo* means heat and *meter* means to measure. Galileo Galilei was one of the earliest inventors of the thermometer.

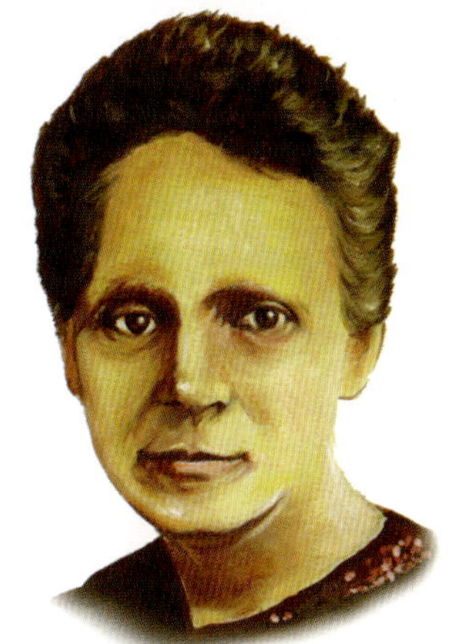

Madam Curie discovered the radioactive elements, Radium and Polonium.

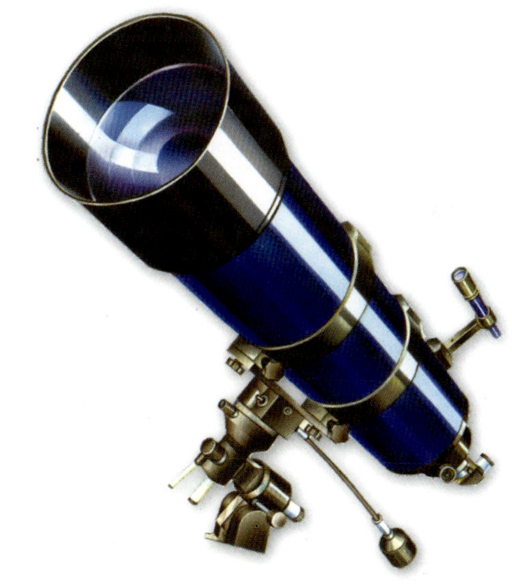

The term "telescope" was first coined by the Greek mathematician Giovanni Demisiani in 1611.

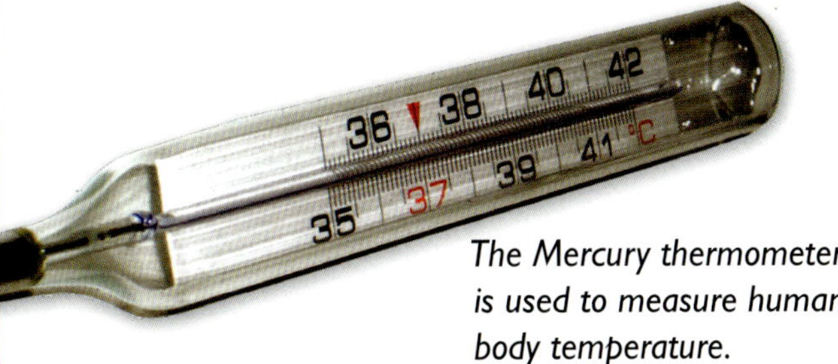

The Mercury thermometer is used to measure human body temperature.

Quick Look

DNA fingerprinting was discovered by Sir Alec Jeffreys in 1984. It was first used in a criminal investigation in the United Kingdom in 1987.

Isaac Newton

Isaac Newton was one of the greatest scientists of his era who is credited with the foundation of modern physical science. Newton formulated the Universal Law of Gravitation and defined the three laws of motion. He used his laws to predict the motions of stars and planets around the sun. Newton also invented the reflecting telescope.

Marie Curie

Marie Curie was a famous scientist who made important discoveries in the field of radioactivity. Marie Curie was the first woman scientist to win a Nobel Prize for discovering polonium and radium in 1903. She also won another Nobel Prize in 1911 for isolating radium and examining its chemical properties. Curie's research was crucial in the development of X-rays.

James Joule

James Prescott Joule was an English scientist who found the relationship between heat, electricity and mechanical work. This relationship came to be known as Joule's Law. Joule also introduced "the mechanical equivalent of heat" by calculating the amount of mechanical work needed to produce an equivalent amount of heat.

Quick Look

Louis Pasteur was a French biologist and chemist. He proposed the germ theory, invented the process of pasteurization and developed vaccines for many diseases.

Isaac Newton was born in Woolsthorpe, Lincolnshire, England on Christmas Day in 1642.

Marie Curie was born in Warsaw, Poland. Her daughter, Irène Joliot-Curie also won a Nobel Prize for Chemistry.

Joule, the SI unit of measuring heat, is named after James Joule.

Albert Einstein

Albert Einstein is one of the most famous scientists of all time. He is best known for his theory of relativity that revolutionised the concepts of time, space, mass and gravitation. Einstein also gave the famous equation $E = mc^2$, which stated that energy and mass are interchangeable and not distinct. This equation became the basis for development of nuclear energy.

Albert Einstein won the 1921 Nobel Prize in Physics.

Benjamin Franklin

Benjamin Franklin was a renowned American scientist and statesman. Franklin gained worldwide fame for his kite experiment that he conducted in 1752. He proved that lightning was a form of electricity. Franklin also invented the lightning rod, Franklin stove, the odometer, armonica and library chair. Franklin is also credited with the creation of the world's first bifocal glasses.

Benjamin Franklin was one of the Founding Fathers of the United States of America.

Wilhelm Roentgen

Wilhelm Roentgen was a famous German physicist who discovered X-rays. His discovery proved very crucial for the medical field as it eased the process of diagnosing disorders or abnormalities inside the human body. Roentgen was the first scientist to receive the first Nobel Prize in Physics in 1901.

The world's first X-ray photograph of a human body was of Wilhelm Roentgen's wife. He created an X-ray photograph of her hand.

Index